TruckingSuccess.com

Dispatch Manual
2020 Edition

A Business Management Manual For The Independent Owner Operator

Dispatch Manual©

2020 Edition
A Comprehensive Resource And Instructions Manual for Independent Owner-Operators

Dispatching Published By

TruckingSuccess.com

Copyright © 2020 – TruckingSuccess.com – All rights reserved. Reproduction in any manner, in whole or in part, without permission is prohibited.

Table of Contents

Introduction

Chapter 1 – Transportation Industry Overview

Chapter 2 – Tools Of The Trade

Chapter 3 – Professionalism

Chapter 4 – Load Availability

Chapter 5 – Finding the Right Loads

Chapter 6 – Booking Loads

Chapter 7 – Freight Handling

Chapter 8 – Freight Delivery

Dear Business Partner:

Congratulations on making the decision to learn more about an important aspect of your trucking business with the goal to maximize your profitability. Also allow me to express our heartfelt gratitude to you for purchasing our Dispatch Manual. We are confident that the knowledge and insights about the transportation industry gained from studying this publication will allow you to work smarter, not harder to succeed as an Owner Operator. It will empower you to make the right choices for your business and give you the confidence to apply this information in your day-to-day operations.

This business publication provides all the tools and information an independent Owner Operator needs to successfully dispatch his or her own truck(s). It explains how to set up your mobile office, lists important business contacts, and provides information about laws and regulations as well as required documents. It describes how to provide excellent customer service, build successful business relationships and effectively manage time and stress. It explains freight volume and facts affecting load availability. It guides you through the process of obtaining your own loads and dispatching your own truck(s). And you also learn about proper freight handling and important delivery procedures. Finally, this publication dispels myths and common misconceptions about the trucking industry, provides you with facts to disprove "truck stop" gossip, and makes the process of dispatching transparent.

Thank you again for choosing our publication "The Dispatch Manual," and best wishes for your success,

The Staff of TruckingSuccess.com

Chapter 1 – Transportation Industry Overview

Professional Organizations

Every industry, trade, profession, and occupation has established business practices and ethical standards that set certain guidelines how business should be conducted. The primary purpose of these practices and standards is to establish trust among the industry to promote good business relationships and facilitate business transactions. The Transport Intermediaries Association (TIA) is the professional and educational organization of the $80.6 billion third party logistics industry, representing transport intermediaries. Among other activities, this organization provides education, research, and services to help its members succeed. The members of TIA include domestic freight forwarders, motor carriers, perishable commodity brokers, logistics management companies, as well as other transportation-related businesses.

The TIA publishes an annual membership directory, which includes freight brokers. As a condition of membership, all TIA members are required to sign and adhere to the TIA Code of Ethics. The Ethics Committee of TIA arbitrates disputes and ensures that members adhere to the Code of Ethics. The articles of the Code of Ethics have been adopted by the TIA to promote and maintain high standards of professional service and ethical business conduct among its members and can be found in the Membership Directory (source: TIA Membership Directory 2014).

Industry Image

Programs such as Trucker Buddy International and Goodyear Highway Hero seek to promote a positive image of the trucking industry among the general public. Nevertheless, widely accepted myths and stereotypes about the trucking industry in general and professional drivers in particular are shaped by popular culture, particularly movies and television series. While some of the stereotypes are positive and portray the trucker as an upstanding and even heroic member of the community, others are negative, such as the portrayal of a tanker truck driver in the motion picture *Thelma and Louise*. Although this is a fictional character, the negative portrayal may contribute to the belief that all drivers behave that way. Unfortunately, the negative perceptions seem to prevail in the general public and the news media perpetrate these stereotypes when reporters unfamiliar with the trucking industry write sensational stories about events involving big rigs without checking the facts. Even industry publications contribute to the misinformation in the industry when they public articles with unsubstantiated information and without providing supporting documentation and facts. Although documentaries such as *Wheels of Change* documenting the how trucking shaped America and *A Mistress Called the Road* portraying the hardships of life on the road are on the market, they fail to reach mass audiences.

Truckers spend a lot of time alone on the road, so they like to socialize when they get to a truck stop or have to wait at a loading dock. Naturally, they talk about their trucks, loads they are pulling, and how much money they are making. Of course, there is nothing wrong with socializing – it is only human to share information. And while you may learn something new once in a while, many times you will hear half-truths or lies that may make you feel bad about your own situation. Only when you know the facts about the trucking industry, will you be able to distinguish the professional drivers from the nonsense talkers. Walk away as soon as you can when you encounter nonsense talkers and do not waste your time to listen to their gossip because you cannot learn anything new from these individuals. You have heard the old adage "time is money" many times, and you have better things to do than trying to educate them.

Dispatch History

Over the past fifteen years, tremendous changes occurred in the way loads are dispatched and how Owner-Operators obtain loads. In the "old" days before the telecommunications and Internet revolution, Owner-Operators usually worked with one or two brokers located in their hometown to obtain loads. After unloading, the trucker went to a nearby truck stop to call his broker for the next load. Some truckers had pagers, but cellular phone were not yet available. Some Owner-Operators also obtained loads from computer load boards found at almost every truck stop throughout the United States. The larger freight brokerage companies posted their loads via a computer network on these load boards and the bigger truck stops had rows of telephone booths so truckers could make their phone calls. Additionally, Owner-Operators called their brokers from the road using pay phones to get load updates or other delivery instructions. When facsimile machines became available at the truck stops in the 1980's, Owner-Operators were able to receive documents on the road. In those days, instant credit checks were not available and truckers relied on expensive publications listing the credit ratings of brokers and carriers. Overall, the pace was slower but more inconvenient.

Owner-Operator Income

Recently, a professional magazine did a cover story about apparently very successful leased- on Owner Operators. One of the truckers featured on the cover of the magazine and profiled in the story told the reporter he expects to gross $350,000.00 in 2014 with a net income of $115,000.00 while he is leased on to a trucking company. To industry insiders, this sounds incredible, but consider the source. The magazine publisher is a trucking company. So, how much money do Owner Operators really earn?

According to published statistics, Owner Operator net income per month from the third quarter of 2013 to the second quarter of 2013 ranged between $4,000.00 and $4,250.00, with a net income per mile between 37 cents to 44 cents. Another Owner Operator profiled in the above- mentioned article expected his take home pay to be $48,000.00 net for 2014, and this figure is realistic. Based on our experience, an independent Owner Operator doing his or her dispatching following our dispatch methods can gross between $180,000.00 to $230,000.00 a year. It is difficult to estimate the annual net income based on the above-mentioned gross income, because operating costs can vary widely. Obviously, an Owner Operator who runs on paid equipment has lower operating costs and costs per mile than a trucker who runs financed equipment. Nevertheless, an Owner Operator averaging 12,000 loaded and empty miles a month should gross $20,000.00 to $22,000.00 a month. These figures are significantly better than published statistics, which show average gross revenue of $10,500.00 to $12,500.00 a month between the third quarter of 2013 and the second quarter of 2013. These income levels are also different when pulling a dry van or a reefer. A dry van will average $1.50 per mile, a reefer should average $1.85 to $2.20 per mile. Always calculate a round trip divided by all miles.

Chapter 2 – Tools Of the Trade

Your Mobile Office

In order to effectively dispatch your truck(s) from the road, you will need the proper tools and space in your truck where you can set up your mobile office. The main components of your office equipments will be a good and sturdy laptop computer with a wireless connection to the Internet, a reliable printer, as well as a quality cellular phone with a good rate plan. For your convenience, you may also invest in a wireless facsimile machine so you can send and receive faxes from brokers and shippers. If a fax machine is not in your budget, you can buy a fax software system that works with your e-mail system, or you can sign up with one of the Internet fax services such as myfax.com and receive faxes via your e-mail account and print them out. You can also use the fax machines at truck stops to send documents requiring your signature to the broker or shipper. Truck stops usually charge $1.00 per page and you may find other businesses such as Kinko's and Office Max that offer the same service at cheaper rates.

Additionally, you will need to set up your business e-mail account, choosing an e-mail address that is professional and reflects your business name. We recommend you also set up a private e-mail account to keep your personal correspondence separate from your business. Also, your voice mail message on your business cell phone should be recorded in a professional manner.

You will also need to designate an area in your truck cabin as your working space and set up a document storage and filing system to keep your paperwork organized. Then you will need the basic office materials such as printer paper, pens, notepapers, paper clips, stapler, hole puncher, and clipboards. Even if you use one of the various routing software programs available for the transportation industry, you should always have a current Rand McNally's Motor Carriers' Road Atlas in your truck.

Important Business Contacts

A variety of organizations, businesses, and governmental agencies provide services, information, products that are vital to the independent Owner Operator and dispatcher. Government agencies such as the Federal Highway Administration promulgate laws, and trucking-related organizations such as the Owner Operator Independent Driver Association (OOID) lobby on behalf of their members and disseminate information via their publication and web sites.

Below is a list of these important business contacts by categories.

Government Agencies

The Federal Motor Carrier Safety Administration (FMCSA) provides background information including license, bond, and insurance information about brokers and motor carriers free of cost.

Federal Motor Carrier
Safety Administration
Washington, D.C.
Phone: (202) 366-9805 (applications)
(202) 385-2423 (insurance) Online: www.li-public.fmcas.dot.gov

The U.S. Department of Agriculture (USDA) also provides on line background checks, including licensing and recent disciplinary actions against brokers free of cost.

U.S. Department of Agriculture
Fruits and Vegetables
Washington, D.C.
Phone: (202) 720-6873
Online: www.ams.usda.gov/fv/paca.htm

The USDA also provides freight rate recommendations on line at http://www.ams.usda.gov/mnreports/wa_fv190.txt

Associations/Organizations

The Owner-Operator Independent Drivers Association publishes a bimonthly/monthly magazine called *Land Line* in addition to providing trucking business consulting, on line background checks, assistance with collections of unpaid freight bills, and attorney referrals. The annual membership fee is $45.00.

Owner-Operator Independent Drivers Association (OOIDA)
P.O. Box 1000
Grain Valley, MO 64029-9900
Phone: (800) 440-5791

The Transportation Intermediaries Association (TIA) is the professional and educational organization of the third party logistics industry, representing transport intermediaries. Among other activities, this organization provides education, research and services to help its members succeed.

The TIA publishes an annual membership directory, which includes a listing of brokers. The directory is on line at www.tianet.org.

Transportation Intermediaries Association
1625 Prince Street, Suite 200
Alexandria, VA 22314-2818
Phone: (703) 299-5700
Fax: (703) 836-0123

The Goodyear Highway Hero Program honors truck drivers who keep the nation's economy moving with daily commerce and who come to the rescue of fellow motorists. Nomination forms and program details may be obtained by calling the Goodyear Highway Hero Hot Line at (330) 796- 8183. The nomination form also is available on the program's web site at www.goodyear.com/ truck/whatsnew/heroes.html.

Services

TruckingSuccess.com provides a variety of services, products and information for the Owner- Operator and the transportation industry. For more information, log on to www.truckingsuccess.com.

RTS Credit Service provides on line background checks on freight brokers using a rating system about each broker's payment habits. RTS charges an annual fee of $299.00 or $35.00 a month for this service. To subscribe, call (888) 492-7006 or go online to www.rtscredit.com.

RBCS Transportation Brokers Rating Service provides business ethics and payment practices on over 4,600 transportation brokers with the RBCS Transportation Brokers Rating Service. RBCS publishes the *Redbook* directory twice a year and also provides broker ratings on line with full access to their website 24/7. For more information, call 1 (800) 252-1925 or go on-line to www.rbcs.com or www.redbooktrucking.com.

FMCSA provides on line background checks, including license, bond and insurance information (see previous section for contact information).

USDA provides on-line background checks, including licensing and recent disciplinary actions, as well as freight rate recommendations (see previous section for contact information).

OOIDA provides a variety of services for the independent Owner-Operator. Please visit OOIDA on-line at www.ooida.com for more details.

RTS Factoring Service offers financial services, which can improve your cash flow and simplify your billing process. To learn more about factoring your Accounts Receivables and to sign up for RTS Factoring Service, please go on-line to www.rtscredit.com .

www.truckersedge.net/promo123 offers a thirty-day free trial of its Internet load board. $34.95 a month after and you may cancel anytime.
Go to: www.truckersedge.net/promo123

Truckstop.com provides trucking business consulting and on-line background checks. The on-line credit check service costs $35.00 a month. For more information call 1 (800) 203-2540 or go on- line to www.truckstop.com.

PostEverywhere.com provides a service, which allows you to post your truck on about twenty-five different on-line load boards. To learn more about this service and to sign up, please go to www.PostEverywhere.com.

Products

TruckingSuccess.com publishes a variety of business manuals and products for independent Owner- Operator trucking operations. To view the product line, please go to: www.truckingsuccess.com.

Wheels of Change video documents how trucking shaped America following the epic adventure of trucks and truckers as they carve their way through a country of unpaved roads, carry the fight in WWII, and haul America into the 21st century. Available at: www.truckingsuccess.com.

A Mistress Called The Road compact disc is a documentary of the life on the road and provides a positive look a the trucking life exploring the powerful pull of the road and subtly reveals its emotional draw in a way only someone who has lived the life could. Available at: www.truckingsuccess.com.

J.J. Keller & Associates, Inc. publishes and sells a variety of trucking-related forms, education materials and business products. For a list of products, please go online to www.truckingsuccess.com and click on the **J.J. Keller icon**.

A variety of companies provide useful services at competitive rates and many offer a thirty- day trial period. TruckingSuccess.com recommends you choose the service that provides you with accurate, timely, and reliable information at a reasonable price.

Professional Publications

TruckingSuccess.com publishes business manuals for the independent Owner-Operator. For more information, please go on-line to www.truckingsuccess.com.

Land Line magazine published by OOIDA (see above for contact information) *Heavy Duty Trucking* magazine – the business magazine of trucking – send subscription inquires or orders to Heavy Duty Trucking, P.O. 16899, North Hollywood, CA 91615, phone (818) 760-0472, online: www.truckinginfo.com

FleetOwner publication provides daily trucking news – to subscribe either to the publication or the newsletter, go to www.FLEETOWNER.COM.

Overdrive magazine published by Randall & Reilly – for subscription inquiries and information call (800) 517-4979 or go on-line to www.overdrive.com.

The Trucker is a semi-monthly national newspaper for the truckload freight industry published by Trucker Publications, Inc., at 1123 S. University, Suite 320, Little Rock, AR 72204-1610. To subscribe, please call (800) 666-2770 or go on-line: www.thetrucker.com.

Laws and Regulations

Broker Registration and Bond: The law requires the Secretary of Transportation to register transportation brokers only if they provide proof of a bond or some other form of approved security. The current broker bond of $75,000.00 was set in 2013.
There are now more than 15,000 brokers and the $75,000.00 bond comes nowhere close to covering the amount of unpaid liabilities incurred by

many brokers today; therefore, thorough broker background checks are an important business tool for the Owner-Operator to avoid nonpayment. It is also important to know that the Federal Motor Carrier Safety Administration does not actively pursue delinquent brokers and brokers who default on their liabilities often do not suffer any consequences and continue their illegal behavior, setting up a new brokerage operation in a different location with a new name.

Broker Contracts: Depending on the clauses of a freight-hauling contract, shippers can be forced to pay twice for the transportation service if a broker does not pay the motor carrier, under Title 49 of the U.S Code. The Transportation Intermediaries Association proposed a new model broker-carrier contract with clauses in the contract such as: "Carrier shall not seek payment from shipper if shipper can prove payment to broker." Owner-Operators signing such contracts waive their rights and remedies under Title 49 of the U.S. Code; therefore, they should carefully read the entire contract to ensure it does not contain clauses detrimental to the Owner-Operators legal rights.

Broker Paperwork: Federal law requires brokers to maintain certain paperwork relating to transportation services brokered and make the paperwork available to the parties involved. According to 49 CFR 371.3, the information requested includes:

- The name, address and registration number of the consigner;
- The bill of lading or freight bill number;
- The amount of compensation received by the broker for the service performed and the name of the payer;
- The amount of compensation for any non-brokerage services and the name of the payer; and
- The amount of freight charges collected and the date collected.

Required Documents

Vendor Set-up Package: The process of booking a load includes completing a set of legal documents and contracts. When you deal with a brokerage firm for the first time, you have to complete a Vendor Set-up Package as well as provide information about your business. Your own package of credentials includes a copy of your Carrier Authority issued by the USDOT/FMCSA, a certificate of liability insurance, a completed W-9 form, and several references.

The Vendor Set-up package includes a data sheet that you must complete, the broker/motor carrier agreement (you must place your initials on every page), the brokerage firm's credentials such as a copies of their Broker's License issued by the Federal Highway Administration, surety bond certificate, certificate of liability insurance, a blank W-9 form, and credit references.

Insurance Certificate: The brokerage firm requires that your insurance company include their firm in your insurance certificate as a Certificate Holder. We advise that you call your insurance company and have them fax the insurance certificate with the name of he Certificate Holder (the brokerage firm) directly to the broker.

Chapter 3 – Professionalism

When you act as your own dispatcher, you will have daily contacts with brokers, agents, insurance company representatives, and shippers. The characteristics that make you a successful Owner-Operator will also contribute to your success in the dispatch business. Excellent customer service skills will help you build good business relationships and establish a good reputation for your business. Effective written communication skills will ensure that your business transactions are processed efficiently and correctly. Furthermore, managing your time effectively to incorporate your dispatch activities into your daily schedule will increase your productivity and profitability.

Customer Service Skills

Almost all of the dispatch activities are conducted over the telephone and via fax machine. Most likely you will never have face-to-face meetings with your business contacts; therefore, it is important that you communicate in a professional manner to make a good first impression. Your verbal communications should be polite and courteous regardless how the other person treats you. Your written communications should be neat and legible, using proper business language and grammar. Avoid coarse and foul language even if you do not get treated right. You should be assertive but not aggressive. If you cannot resolve a conflict in a professional manner, consider not doing business with a company that does not treat you with respect, rather than getting into verbal arguments over the telephone.

Building Business Relationships

Good verbal and written communications skills will help you establish productive business relationships and ensure your business transactions are handled properly. All business relationships are built on mutual trust and the understanding that the parties involved live up to their respective responsibilities. As such, you should conduct your business dealings with integrity and fairness, following through and honoring all of your business agreements. Again, if you have a bad experience with a company who does not follow generally accepted business practices; it is better not to do business with them. However, keep in mind that at times when you call a brokerage company about a specific problem, you may speak with an individual who is poorly trained and does not have the necessary expertise to assist you. In this case, do not waste valuable time explaining your situation because this individual will not be able to resolve the particular issue. In our experience, this happens often during weekends and after regular business hours. Most large brokerage companies maintain twenty-four-hour service, but the agents available after regular business hours are not as experienced and familiar with the specifics of your load as your broker/ agent. Rather than wasting your time and getting frustrated with an agent who is unable to help you, we suggest you wait and call your broker/agent the next morning to resolve the issue properly.

In the competitive transportation industry, maintaining friendly business relationships with brokers may make a difference during times when loads are scarce or rates are down. We recommend you create a telephone contact list of all the companies and brokers with whom you have established positive business relationships. You will find that over time this list will be a very valuable business asset.

When you negotiate financial details such as freight rates, detention pay, fuel surcharges, payment for additional stops, and mileage pay for dead-heading, you should always keep the "bigger picture" in mind to avoid getting "hung up" on minor financial details. Often inexperienced Owner-Operators lose good loads or valuable time over minor financial differences. For example, the standard rate for overnight detention time is $250.00. Although an Owner-Operator may feel that (s)he should receive a higher pay for their valuable time and ask for $400.00 or $500.00, it is useless to argue this point with the shipper or broker, because they will not pay more than the current standard rate. It makes more business sense to accept this reality and move on to the next load. Remember, you only produce revenue when the wheels of your truck are turning.

Providing excellent customer service also helps to establish and maintain good business relationships. Owner-Operators who provide good service develop a good reputation over time and generate good will. The basic elements of service include picking up and delivering loads on time, following delivery instructions, making required check-in calls, and communicating any unforeseen delays to the other party.

Time Management

Finding the right load(s) takes time, experience, and some planning. When you dispatch your own truck from the road, you will have to fit your dispatch activities into your daily driving routine; however, eventually you will work out a system that will fit your travel schedules. To complicate matters more, you have to take into consideration time zones, regular business hours, as well as your delivery schedules.

We recommend that you schedule a one-hour stop about every two days during the morning hours to review on-line load boards and make phone calls. You should call brokerage companies between 9:00 AM and 11:00 AM their local time because everybody is in the office during the morning hours taking care of business. In our experience, most load-booking business is done before lunch breaks. After lunch, you may place courtesy calls to brokers/agents to advise them that your truck is available so they may call you when loads become available later in the day or the next morning. To avoid costly layovers and waiting time at the loading dock, you must book your loads in advance, not on the day you unload at your destination. This means you should start searching for a new load three days prior to unloading your current load. If you cannot find a good- paying load on the first day, you still have two days left to research load boards and call brokers.

Stress Management

Life on the road is already stressful without the added dispatch duties.
What can you do to make it all work? There are several steps you can take to reduce stress and accomplish your daily tasks successfully. Planning ahead and establishing a daily schedule and adhering to it will help you stay on track. Utilize the organizational system you devised when you set up your mobile office and prioritize tasks to effectively manage your time. Having a place for everything and putting it back where it belongs when you no longer use it will save you time every day. As you gain more experience with your dispatching duties, it will become part of your daily routine. In summary, experience, planning ahead and adhering to a daily schedule as well as maintaining an organizational system will help you avoid stressful situations. What may your daily schedule look like when you are on the West Coast? You unloaded at 4:00 AM and are headed to a truck stop where you arrive at 5:00 AM. You freshen up and eat breakfast. From approximately 6:00 AM to :00 AM., you scan on-line load boards and make phone calls to shippers and brokers to secure a load when you arrive at your next location. Following the Hours of Service regulations, you sleep ten hours. Then you drive to pick up your next load at 6:00 PM.

Chapter 4 – Load Availability

How many times have you wondered why you sit empty at a truck stop for several days before your broker finds another load for you and why you do not get the high-paying loads other truckers boast about hauling all the time? You may have guessed it -- there are no simple answers to your questions! Only when you gain insight into how the transportation industry works will you understand how the business principle of supply and demand affects how much a load pays and how many loads are available at any given time.

Freight Volume

Cyclicality: Although there are tens of thousands of loads available at any given day, economic cycles and seasonal demand determine the volume of available freight. When the economy expands rapidly, freight volume increases and lots of loads are available at very good rates because shippers compete for tight truckload capacity. On the contrary, when the economy slows down and contracts, freight volume decreases and rates go down. The American Trucking Association tracks for-hire truck tonnage and issues a quarterly Truck Tonnage Index for the trucking industry.

Economic Activity: Some economic activities generate more freight volume than others. Construction, manufacturing and even international trade depend on trucking to transport raw materials, manufactured goods, and merchandise. In fact, trucks move about seventy percent of all domestic freight, including wholesale and retail goods. Strong consumer spending on high-ticket items, food, clothing and other goods has a positive effect on freight volume. When interest rates and gas prices are high, consumer spending drops, resulting in a weaker freight volume but increased transportation capacity and lower freight rates.

Seasonal Demand in addition to cyclical changes in freight levels, seasonal demand affects the freight volume and rates. Every year, during the peak growing season in California, thousands of Owner-Operators head toward the West Coast for the high- paying produce loads to the East Coast. Word about $6,000.00 produce loads to the East Coast spreads like wildfire and soon there is a glut of trucks on the West Coast. What is the result? Rates drop immediately due to excessive truck capacity. Shippers now can choose between numerous carriers who accept almost any rate just to get out of California. As a result, loads that paid $6,000.00 one week, go for $4,000.00 to $5,000.00 the next week.

Generally, demand for freight capacity changes with the seasons. From January to April, demand is slow. It picks up when the produce season starts on the West Coast and peaks during the early summer. Freight volume slows down again after the Fourth of July, picks up again in the fall and remains strong during the pre-holiday months and through the Christmas rush.

Freight Volume by States: Additionally, location affects the volume of available freight. The Top 15 Activity States based on incoming and outgoing loads posts are Texas, Ohio, Illinois, Pennsylvania, California, Georgia, Indiana, Florida, North Carolina, Tennessee, New York, Maryland, Missouri, Michigan, Wisconsin, and Arkansas. However, some states such as Texas, Pennsylvania, Georgia, Florida, and North Carolina have more incoming than outgoing loads. That means if you deliver a load into these states, you will have a difficult time finding a suitable outgoing load. On the other hand, some states such as Ohio, Illinois, New York, Wisconsin, Arkansas, and Indiana have more outgoing than incoming loads. That means if you deliver a load into these states you will easily find a good outgoing load in these states. States such as California, Tennessee, Missouri, and Michigan have a relatively balanced ratio of incoming and outgoing loads. The Top 15 Activity States Index is published in the *Heavy Duty Trucking* magazine.

Equipment

In addition to the above-mentioned factors, the type of equipment an Owner-Operator owns and operates narrows or widens the pool of freight that is available at any given day, and it determines how much revenue (s)he generates throughout the business year. Most Owner-Operators choose what type of equipment they prefer to operate at the beginning of their career and specialize in either flatbed, step deck, tanker truck, dry van or refrigerated van transportation. Each equipment type has its own drawbacks as well as advantages. The rates for flatbed and step deck freight are very good; however, it is often difficult to find connecting loads without having to "deadhead" hundreds of miles. Step deck freight also often requires special tarps and expensive safety equipment.

Independent Owner-Operators generally do not operate tanker trucks for obvious reasons
– the type of freight they can haul is too restricted. Although dry vans have been very popular, it is difficult to make a living hauling dry freight because the rate is often less than $1.00 a mile, which is below the cost-per-mile for many Owner-Operators. The fifty-three-foot refrigerated van or "reefer" is the most versatile equipment for the independent Owner-Operator. It can handle dry, refrigerated, and frozen freight, making it easier to find suitable loads anywhere and anytime. However, it takes skill and experience to handle perishable cargo properly so it does not sustain damage in transit.

Owner-Operator Specifics

Finally, the Owner-Operator's personal preferences as well as business parameters determine how many loads (s)he can select from the large pool of available freight. Personal preferences include weather conditions, length of time away from home, and family obligations. Less experienced drivers may prefer to stay on the southern routes during the winter months rather than going to the Midwest and Northeast where there is a change of running into snow and ice. Family obligations are also a consideration and determine how long an Owner-Operator is willing to stay out on the road and away from home. Business considerations such as permits, cost per mile, Hours of Service, and a shipper's credit worthiness affect load selection and trip planning. An Owner-Operator who has permits for all forty-eight states will have a wider selection of freight than an Owner-Operator who only runs in the eleven Western States. Cost-permile calculations will eliminate many of the loads offered because it is not profitable to haul cheap loads and a shipper's credit rating will further narrow the pool of available loads.

Hours of Service Regulations

Furthermore, delivery time frames of loads that are deemed suitable have to fit into the Owner-Operator's Hours of Service schedule. This requires a calculation of distance and daily miles to delivery time frames. When an Owner-Operator has been on duty for almost sixty hours in seven consecutive days or seventy hours in eight consecutive days, it will not make any sense to book a cross-country load with a tight delivery schedule. In this case, the Owner-Operator should post the truck and inform his or her contacts that (s)he is available to take the next load after having been thirty-four or more consecutive hours off-duty.

Chapter 5 – Finding the Right Loads

Freight Rates

The state of the economy, seasonal demand, physical location, and transportation capacity affect freight rates at any given day. Generally, rates for cross-country loads from the West to the East Coast are $1.85 to $2.20 per mile or $5,550 to $6,600.00 for the entire trip. However, rates for loads originating on the East Coast and going to the West Coast are thirty to forty percent lower than loads originating on the West Coast and going to the East Coast. Generally, rates for cross- country loads from the East to the West Coast are $1.25 to $1.65 per mile or $3,750.00 to $4,950.00 for the entire trip. In some states such as Florida or Texas rates for outgoing loads are $1.30 or less because of excessive transportation capacity in these locations. Many Owner-Operators are not aware of a state's incoming/outgoing rate differential and accept these cheap long-haul loads just to get out of these states. They haul these loads without making any profit because the cost per mile for most Owner-Operators is now $1.20 and they may even lose some of the profit from the better- paying load they brought into the state. Only the shippers will benefit and the Owner-Operator may barely break even.

Positioning

Often an Owner-Operator may locate a good-paying load to a suitable destination, but (s)he is several hundred miles away from the pickup location. This poses a challenge but there are several options for handling this situation. One option is to continue researching the load boards and perhaps locate another load with a nearby pickup location. However, additional research may not yield another suitable load and the original load is the best offer available at the time. In this case you may chose the second option, which involves dead-heading to the pickup destination, but driving empty and without pay is not the most economical solution considering today's high fuel prices. The third and more practical option involves finding a short-haul load to the area where the good-paying load is located. In this scenario, the Owner-Operator may intentionally book one of these cheap loads for a short haul only to position the truck in a location where (s)he can pick up a better-paying load.

Round-trip Concept

Considering all these factors, how do you find loads that pay well and increase your revenue? First you have to change your approach and adopt a new strategy. Instead of using a load-by-load approach, you should adopt the **round-trip concept** to determine if load rates meet your criteria. The round trip calculation only works when you dispatch your own truck because it requires planning ahead. To do it right, you take a load cross-country from the West to the East Coast and you split the return trip into two or three sections.

Below is an example of dispatching using the round-trip concepts to enhance your revenue.

1. Start in California with a load to Massachusetts
   Approx. 3,000 miles at $2.00 per mile
   $6,000.00
1. Next take a load from Massachusetts to Ohio
   Approx. 400 miles at $1.20 per mile
   $480.00
1. Next take a load from Ohio to Colorado
   Approx. 1,400 miles at $1.60 per mile
   $2,240.00
1. Complete round-trip with a load from Colorado to California
   Approx. 1,200.00 at $1.35 per mile
   $1,620.00

Total revenue for cross-country roundtrip   **$10,340.0**

Comparison Trip

1	Start in California with a load to Massachusetts Approx. 3,000 miles at $2.00 per mile	$6,000.00
2	Backhaul load to California Approx. 3,000 miles at $1.10 per mile	$3,300.00

Total revenue for cross-country roundtrip $9,300.00

Difference $1,040.00

The Owner-Operator who took the straight back-haul to California earned $1,040.00 less on one round-trip. If he makes two round-trips a month, he will lose $2,080.00 of revenue per month, or $24,960.00 of revenue in one year.

Even if you haul freight only in certain regions of the United States, always calculate the round-trip revenue to determine if a load is acceptable. You will be more flexible in your decision-making using this approach and it may avoid argument about freight rates with brokers and shippers.

Load Resources

Load Boards: Modern communications technology has simplified access to load information. Independent Owner-Operators only need a computer (laptop) and (wireless)

Internet to view thousands of load listings on on-line load boards every day. Among the dozens of on-line load boards, getloaded.com and truckstop.com are the more popular services among Owner-Operators. These load board companies charge a fee of approximately $30.00 per month and may offer a thirty-day trial period at no cost. The load boards also provide credit ratings, but they are not always accurate.

Post Your Own Truck: When you sign up with an on-line load board, you can also post your own truck days in advance of your next delivery destination so brokers and shippers can call you about loads they have available when you arrive at your destination. You will get calls with freight offers and you may even receive a good-paying load without much effort of your own, saving you valuable time researching suitable loads. You may also utilize services such as PostEverywhere.com, which automatically submits your truck information to approximately twenty-five on-line load boards. When you use these services, you should always post your truck after you get loaded so the information is available on-line two to three days before you deliver the current load and your truck is empty again. This allows you to plan ahead and make use of the round-trip dispatch system.

Brokers and Logistics Companies: In addition to the on-line load resources, honest brokers and third-party logistics companies continue to be valuable contacts for obtaining loads. Most of the larger brokerage and logistics companies offer various payment options including quick pay, which may be to the Owner-Operator's advantage. The Transportation Intermediaries Association (TIA) publishes an annual membership directory, which lists hundreds of brokers who have undergone background checks and adhere to the TIA's Code of Ethics. Large brokerage firms and logistics companies generate loads through their national and international contacts. Their offices usually operate twenty-four hours a day, seven days a week. When you establish business relationships, start creating your own contact and reference list of companies that you found reliable and credit worthy so you can use their services again without doing additional credit checks.

Shipper-Direct Loads: Many carriers would like to get loads directly from shippers and eliminate the middleman who takes a cut from the freight rate. While it is not impossible for independent Owner-Operators to work directly with shippers, it is a difficult undertaking because most shippers prefer to work with larger carriers. One reason is that the shippers are able to negotiate better rates with the carrier for large freight volume, and the carrier guarantees that the shipper's loads get picked up and delivered. Even when an Owner-Operator finds shipper-direct loads, they are only one-way and (s)he still has to use a broker for the back-haul load. However, the financial aspects of shipper-direct loads will break the deal for most Owner-Operators. Shippers generally pay in sixty to ninety days! In the capital-intensive transportation industry where thousands of dollars are at stake with every load, sixty to ninety days is too long to wait for payment for most Owner-Operators. Should the shipper experience financial difficulties and be unable to pay, the Owner-Operator faces financial ruin.

Researching Loads

Perusing on-line load boards is the first step in researching loads to determine what freight is available to tentative destinations. Make sure you ignore all listings without credit ratings as well as credit ratings below 90. A credit listing of "N/A" indicates the company listing the load is new and has not established a credit history. Entering into a business relationship with such companies is a high risk because they have no payment history to ensure you get paid. And if you factor your freight bills, the factoring company will not accept your paperwork. Companies with credit ratings between 85 and 100 are considered low risk because they have established a financial track record of paying their freight bills. Companies with credit ratings below 85 present a moderate to high financial risk and Owner-Operators doing business with these companies may have difficulty collecting their freight bills.

The next step is making phone calls to get more details from the broker or agent about potential loads you selected from on-line load boards. While the broker gives you the load information over the phone, you must make your assessment based on the factors discussed in the previous chapters to determine if it is a "good" load. The load information includes details about the number of pickups and drops; pickup location, date and time; delivery location, date and time; the type of product, total weight, freight rate, as well as other shipping instructions, and the shipper's Motor Carrier identification number. Be aware that you only have a few seconds to decide if you want to haul a particular load. If you cannot make up your mind right away and you call back later, the load will no longer be available because you are one of many Owner-Operator inquiring about the same loads.

In case you do not find suitable loads on-line, you must start calling brokerage and logistics firms to determine what freight is available to your tentative destination. If you have already established your own contact list, first call your own contacts and check what loads they have available. And, if you posted your truck on-line, you should also be getting calls with freight offers. If your own contacts do not result in a load, then move on to the TIA broker list. Be aware there are some days where it is extremely difficult to find a load despite all your efforts. When this is the case, stop calling and continue working your dispatch system again the next day.

Over time, you will gain the experience to determine quickly if a load is a "good load" considering all the factors previously discussed. Never simply rely on a broker or agent's word and always follow the proper background and credit check procedure to make sure you are dealing with a financially stable company. Owner-Operators all over the United States have lost millions of dollars in freight revenue to unscrupulous brokers and shippers.

TruckingSuccess.com has compiled a listing of reliable and ethical brokerage companies that have a good payment history and high credit rating. This listing is included as an appendix to the dispatch manual to help you get started with the understanding that you verify credit ratings and payment history again when you do business with these companies. TruckingSuccess.com cannot guarantee the credit ratings and does not accept legal liability if a company's credit history has changed.

Chapter 6 – Booking Loads

Booking Process

After you verbally agreed via telephone to haul a load and the broker/agent gave you all the pertinent information, you must complete the required paperwork. As stated in Chapter 2, the process of booking a load includes completing a set of legal documents and contracts. When you deal with a brokerage firm for the first time, you have to complete a Vendor Set-up Package, which will be faxed to you, as well as provide information about your business. Your own package of credentials includes a copy of your Carrier Authority issued by the USDOT/FMCSA, a certificate of liability insurance, a completed W-9 form, and several references. You must fax copies of your own credentials along with the completed Vendor Set-up Package to the brokerage firm's designated fax number.

The Vendor Set-up package includes a data sheet that you must complete, the broker/motor carrier agreement (you must place your initials on every page), the brokerage firm's credentials such as a copies of their broker's license issued by the Federal Highway Administration, surety bond certificate, certificate of liability insurance, a blank W-9 form, and credit references. To complete the three-page data sheet, you simply fill in the requested contact information and complete the checklist for required information, and requested information.

Usually, the brokerage firm requires that your insurance company include their firm in your insurance certificate as a Certificate Holder. We advise that you call your insurance company and have them fax the insurance certificate with the name of he Certificate Holder (the brokerage firm) directly to the broker. This will speed up the process of receiving the fax with your rate confirmation sheet signed by the broker. Then, you must sign the rate confirmation sheet and fax it back to the broker (make sure you file the most current rate confirmation sheet because you must submit it later to receive your settlement). Overall, this entire process takes about one to two hours.

If your rate confirmation rate has not arrived after one hours, most likely you are dealing with an unprofessional agent and/or the shipper has not given the okay for the load and the broker wants to hold your truck hoping (s)he gets the load. When you get the impression that the broker/ agent is playing games with you, abandon this load and start searching for another one.

Once you have established business relationships with brokerage companies and/or other logistics companies, the subsequent process of booking loads will be easier and faster because they have your information in their database. After you agreed on a rate for a particular load, the only paperwork involved is the rate confirmation sheet, which the broker/agent will fax to you to sign and then fax it back. Occasionally, circumstances arise that require changes or modifications of the original agreement; e.g., adding lumper fees to the freight rate. Whenever there are changes to the agreed-upon transportation contract, you must request and receive a signed updated rate confirmation sheet because you will be paid according to the information on the rate confirmation sheet.

Credit Check

Before you finalize the booking process, you must complete a credit check to get first-hand information about the company's payment history. Credit services use a rating system to classify a company's creditworthiness. RTS Credit Service uses alphabetical letters A through F to rate a broker's payment history. A rating of A is the best score a company or broker can achieve while a rating of F is the worst score. Brokers with A, B, or C credit ratings are financially stable and pay their bills. Brokers with D, E, or F credit ratings pose a financial risk and you should not do business with them. Even after you have established a business relationship with a shipper or carrier, you should complete a credit check every two to three months to ensure the company's financial stability and payment practices have not deteriorated. In the capital-intensive transportation industry, a company's financial condition can change quickly when a creditor defaults and Owner-Operators cannot afford to not get paid for their services. The six-digit Motor Carrier identification number also provides clues about a company's financial history. Established companies have lower motor carrier identification numbers; that is, the first three digits of the MC number are in the 100's or 200's such as 101812 or 219322. Companies or brokers with higher Motor

Carrier numbers where the first three digits are in the 500's to 700's such as 811225 or 954195 are relatively new and may not have established good credit ratings.

Contract Specifics

After you completed all the paperwork involved in booking the load, you must review the contract to ensure it reflects the agreed-upon specifics. Should you discover discrepancies, request a correction of the erroneous information and have an updated rate confirmation sheet and contract faxed to you for your signature.

Freight Rate: This reflects the agreed-upon amount that the Owner-Operator will receive for hauling a particular load. It may also include reimbursements for lumper fees, detention pay, or payment for "deadhead" miles, as well as payment for multiple pick-ups and drops.

Lumper Fees: Federal law states that the shipper is financially responsible for the unloading costs and must reimburse the Owner-Operator for lumping fees. Nowadays, lumping services charge between $80.00 and $140.00 to unload a full trailer. The contract should contain a clause specifying that the Owner-Operator is paid for lumping fees and the method of payment; e.g., by Com-check or reimbursement after the receipt is submitted.

Detention Pay: Federal law does not regulate compensation for waiting time at the loading dock. The prevailing sentiment by regulatory agencies is to let the marketplace sort out how the Owner-Operator is compensated for delays at the loading docks. Nevertheless, most large brokerage companies now pay detention time after a grace period of four to five hours. The industry standard for detention pay is $250.00 for a twenty-four-hour period. It should be a standard clause of every contract of haul. Review your contracts to ensure they contain a clause pertaining to detention pay.

Financial Settlement

Quick Pay: Most brokerage companies offer several payment options including Quick Pay, which means payment is made either within twenty-four hours or seven days after the Owner-Operator submits the signed bill of lading, rate confirmation sheet, and invoice. Companies offering the service charge a service fee between 3 percent and 5 percent for making the payment within twenty-four hours. For a freight bill of $4,000.00 a 3% fee amounts to $120.00. For payment in seven days, most companies charge a fee of 1% to 2%.

In most cases, the Quick Pay option is listed on the rate confirmation sheet, and the Owner- Operator must check that box to receive Quick Pay as well as note it on the invoice (s)he submits. Some companies require that the Owner-Operator signs up for Quick Pay in advance and then all invoices are processed and paid using the Quick Pay option. Payment is made either with a regular business check mailed to the OwnerOperator's business address or the Owner-Operator can request a Com-check.

Advances: Most companies still offer advances and issue Com-checks to Owner-Operators to cover fuel costs. The amount of the advance depends on the freight rate. Companies charge a 2% fee based on the face amount of the Com-check as well as $25.00 for the cost of the Com-check.

Reimbursements: Most companies issue Com-checks for lumper fees; however, there are exceptions. Some companies require that the Owner-Operator submit the lumper receipt for reimbursement.

Factoring: Factoring companies charge a service fee between 3% to 5% of the freight bill and pay within twenty-four to forty-eight hours after receiving the invoice and required documents. Before you sign up with a factoring service, obtain a sample contract and study the complete document carefully.

Bill of Lading: In order to get paid, the Owner-Operator must submit the bill of lading signed by the receiver, the rate confirmation sheet, and an invoice to the brokerage company. Some companies have specific procedures and designated fax numbers for billings. The Owner-Operator must follow the company's procedure to ensure your paperwork is processed properly and you receive your payment without delay.

Chapter 7 – Freight Handling

Loading

Proper freight handling is a crucial step in the dispatch and transportation chain because the Owner-Operator only receives payment when the freight arrives at its destination on time and without damage. After the freight booking process is completed, the Owner-Operator switches "gears" from being a dispatcher to transportation professional by driving to the designated pickup location, arriving there at the scheduled loading time, and making sure the freight is properly loaded on the trailer.

While at the loading dock, the Owner-Operator must supervise the loading process. That means (s)he must check the paperwork to ensure (s)he picks up the right load because sometimes load numbers get mixed up or the same load number is given to different loads. If there are problems with the load number or other issues arise, the broker must be contacted to clarify the matter. Then (s)he must estimate the total weight by counting the number of pallets and multiplying that number with the weight per pallet to ensure the trailer is not over weight, because there are stiff fines imposed for loads exceeding the maximum weight limit of 80,000 pounds. The Owner-Operator also must instruct the warehouse personnel how to place the pallets on the trailer to ensure proper weight distribution on the axles. That means less-heavy product has to go into the nose of the trailer, the heavier product into the middle section, and less-heavy product again in the tail section. This can be accomplished with the following load distribution pattern: two single, one double, and a single pallet in the trailer nose, the heavier pallets in the middle, and one or two single and one double pallet in the trailer tail. Finally, the total weight must be verified at an official scale.

The Owner-Operator also has to take into consideration that warehouse personnel do not necessarily care about him or her or their truck and trailer. This is a sad but true fact, and forklift operators frequently cause damage to the trailer and/or the product. These careless actions result in costly repairs or deductions from the freight rate; therefore, the Owner-Operator must supervise the loading process and visibly inspect and count the product as it gets loaded onto the trailer to ensure no damage is done to either the product or the trailer or shortages occur.

Securing Shipment

After successfully completing the loading process at the warehouse, the Owner-Operator must secure the freight to prevent damage during transit. Although some minor movement of the product will occur during the transport, significant shifting must be prevented. That means load locks must be installed to keep pallets and product in place, and other required protective material such as airbags must be placed between pallet stacks. Pallet jacks and unused pallets must be secured properly so they do not cause damage to the freight. The trailer must be locked and should not be left unattended for extended periods of time during the transportation process to avoid theft, damage, and pilferage. When the freight consists of high-ticket items, shippers may place a seal on the trailer door; therefore, it is important that the load is secured before the seal is installed.

Refrigerated Product

The Owner-Operator must take extra-special care throughout the entire transportation process when (s)he transports perishable products such as produce, vegetables, and fruit. The Owner-Operator must be familiar with the trailer's refrigeration system to ensure it keeps the trailer and its contents at the required temperature. Temperature checks must be conducted twice a day to verify the "reefer" operates correctly. Prior to loading, the trailer must be inspected for damage to the cooling system, and the integrity of the trailer body verified. Sometimes the air ducts in the ceiling are damaged during loading or unloading, resulting in uneven distribution of cool air in the trailer, which could result in part of the product receiving either not enough or too much refrigeration. Leaks in the trailer's wall, ceiling, or floor may also compromise the effectiveness of the refrigeration system. In either case, the product will spoil and the receiver will reject the shipment, resulting in an insurance claim against the Owner-Operator and (s)he will not receive payment for transportation.

Prior to loading perishable products, the trailer must be pre-cooled for at least thirty minutes and the product must be pre-cooled before loading as well. The Owner-Operator must check the product's temperature to make sure it is not warm when it is brought into the trailer. You must also make sure the trailer doors remain closed before loading and are closed immediately after all product is loaded on the trailer. When you arrive at your destination, you must make sure the product is promptly unloaded after the trailer doors are opened.

Frozen Product

Frozen product must be handled with the same care as refrigerated loads to make sure the product remains frozen and does not spoil. Again, temperature checks must be conducted twice a day to verify the "reefer" operates correctly.

The aforementioned handling instructions for refrigerated and frozen products are general guidelines based on many years of experience hauling refrigerated and frozen loads, and TruckingSuccess.com cannot be held legally liable for product loss. In addition to properly maintaining and servicing the refrigeration unit, the Owner-Operator must follow the operating instructions for the refrigeration equipment (s)he operates and adhere to the shipper's written instructions with regard to product handling.

Chapter 8 – Freight Delivery

Delivery Instructions

In addition to delivery instructions provided by the broker, the Owner-Operator must check the bill of lading for specific instructions and ensure (s)he understands and adheres to the specific requirements such as daily check-in calls and calling ahead to set up a delivery appointment. When daily check-in calls are required, it is important not to miss them and to make the calls at the required time, providing pertinent information about the load to the broker. However, in certain areas of the country cell phones do not work due to a lack of transmission towers, making it difficult to comply with the call-in requirements. In this case, you must call in as soon as you move into an area with cellular reception. It is equally important to call and scheduled the delivery appointment in advance to avoid waiting time and delays at the delivery dock.

Directions, Delays, Troubleshooting

Although routing software and driving direction programs such as Map Quest are available to obtain directions, you should not exclusively rely on these modern technological conveniences because they are not 100% reliable. When you deliver to an unfamiliar location, you should get directions to your delivery destination from the broker and/or receiver. As an Owner-Operator, you must carry in your truck a road atlas designed for the transportation industry and use it to plan the most efficient route to your destination. Detours and delays as a result of "bad" directions waste time, fuel and money. Occasionally, delays are inevitable due to factors beyond the Owner-Operators control. There may be accidents, road construction, or delays due to bad weather. In any case, you should adjust your daily driving schedule to include such delays without impacting your final delivery time.

When the Owner-Operator experiences breakdowns and equipment failure of the truck trailer, the situation becomes more critical and troubleshooting skills are essential to return the equipment into working order and reach the destination in time. The Owner-Operator must have some technical understanding to determine how to handle a breakdown. If it is a relatively minor problem, (s)he may be able to repair or at least temporarily fix the problem in order to get to the next truck stop or repair shop. If it is a major technical problem, a mobile repair service may be able to complete the repair or the truck and trailer may have to be towed. When it becomes obvious that the breakdown will result in a significant delivery delay, the Owner-Operator must contact the broker and advise of the situation so that either a new delivery date may be set or arrange for alternative transportation if there is a risk of product loss.

Delivery & Bill of Lading

The Owner-Operator must arrive at the scheduled delivery time to avoid delays, unnecessary waiting at the dock, and potential rejection of the load. Should (s)he experience excessive delays with unloading nevertheless or other complications at the destination, the broker must be informed immediately about the situation so (s)he can intervene and straighten out the matter. The Owner-Operator must also supervise the unloading process to ensure neither the product nor the trailer are damaged by careless warehouse personnel (please see Chapter 7 for more details), and load locks or other equipment is not stolen. If lumpers are used to unload, the Owner-Operator must obtain a Com-check to pay the fee and a receipt for documentation. In case the Owner-Operator used his or own pallets during the loading process, the pallets must be exchanged.

After the successful completion of the unloading process, the Owner-Operator must obtain a signature on the bill of lading so it can be submitted for payment along with the rate confirmation sheet. Finally, the trailer must be steam-cleaned to avoid possible contamination of the next load.

Rejected Loads

Load rejection is the worst-case scenario of the delivery process and it occurs quite often with produce loads. The load my be rejected for legitimate reasons when the product is spoiled due to improper handling during transit or late delivery; however, many times it appears "games" are being played at the expense of the Owner-Operator and shipper. This can happen when the receiver ordered too much product or does not have enough storage space to unload the product. Regardless of the circumstances, when it appears a load is being rejected, the Owner-Operator must be vigilant to ensure no tampering with the load occurs, such as pulling pallets off the truck and letting them sit at the dock, and the broker must be notified immediately. Also, the federal inspector must be notified to inspect the product and issue an inspection report.

Appendix

Brokerage Companies By State, Recommended on the Basis of Years in Business and By Credit Ratings:

The Brokerage Firms Pay Between 10 and 30 days after Receipt of BOL and they also have Advances and Quick Pay Options Available.

Before accepting a load check your cost per mile, don't pay the broker and haul cheap loads.

Alabama

G & P Distributing, Inc., Albertville, AL P: 800-374-3067 F: 256-891-9764 loads from GA to west coast

C2 Freight Resources, Houston, AL P: 888-371-5335 F: 205-489-5326 loads from OH to TX.

McAlpin Transportation, Inc., Vinemont, AL P: 877-253-4457 F: 256-739-9390 loads in 48 states, Canada and Mexico.

Arizona

Best Freight, LLC, Buckeye, AZ   P: 623-386-4266 F: 623-386-4571 loads from TX or east coast to AZ - loads from AZ to 48 states -loads from north west to AZ.

Crossroad Transportation, Mesa, AZ   P: 800-777-9830 F 480-991-5740 loads in 48 states and out of west coast.

Bigelow Truck Brokers, Inc. Glendale, AZ P: 623-931-5955 F: 623-931-7131 loads from AZ to east coast and 11 western states.

All American Carriers, Glendale, AZ P: 623-842-4460 F: 623-842-4539 loads from CA to east and east to west.

Freightmatchers.com, Glendale, AZ P: 602-237-6718 F: 623-321-9288 loads from CA to 48 states.

Greenway Transportation Service, Inc. Scottsdale, AZ P: 800-528-4025 and 480-443-8800 Fax: 480-998-9440 - loads from AZ to east coast.

Advantage Transport, Phoenix, AZ P: 800-444-0808 and 602-331-0808 F: 800-516-0975 loads from 11 western states and south east and northeast.

Arkansas

ABF Freight, Fort Smith, AR P: 877-279-8090 F: 479-494-8129
loads from north east to south east.

Willis Shaw Express, Inc., Elm Springs, AR P: 877-405-1298 F: 479-248-1967 loads from 48 states.

Stallion Transportation Group, Beebe, AR P: 800-597-2425 F: 501-882-1588 loads from 48 states

Addison Transportation, Cabot, AR P: 800-580-6560 F: 501-843-7279 loads from 48 states.

BNSF Logistics LLC, Springdale, AR P: 800-941-0724 F: 479-587-7254
loads from east to west.

Jerry Dudley, Inc., Fayettsville, AR P: 800-221-0723 loads from DE to CA -US- Mail – loads from IL to 48 states.

California

Allen Lund Company, Inc., La Canada, CA   P: 800-777-6142   F: 800-434-5863 loads from 48 states.

RLT, Inc. Redding, CA   P: 800-824-4121   F: 530-241-7084 loads from Nogales, AZ to WA, OR, CA

Bowers Trucking, Oroville, CA P: 800-821-0545 F: 530-534-8878 loads from 48 states.

LLR Logistics, LLC, Monrovia, CA   P: 866-236-2275   F: 626-447-0294 loads from IA to UT.

American Freightways, San Diego, CA   P: 866-326-5902   F: 858-217-3305 loads from CA to east coast.

Cargo Master, Inc., Lake Elsinore, CA   P: 800-683-750

Diversified Transportation Services, Torrance, CA P: 800-460-8540 F: 310-436-1970 loads from 48 states and international.

Colorado

CR England, Greeley, CO   P: 800-321-5966   F: 970-330-4500 loads from TX to CO.

Timberline Freight Service, Evergreen, CO   P: 1-800-495-9102 F: 303-674-9104 loads from OK-TX-Panhandle to west and north-west 17 states.

Olathe Trucking, LLC, Denver, CO   P: 888-627-0121   F: 303-573-0663 loads from CO to 11 western states.

Freight Logistics, Inc., Denver, CO   P: 800-575-3346   F: 720-377-9463 loads from 48 states.

Connecticut

United Express Service, Inc., Rocky Hill, CT P: 860-529-7737 F: 860-721-7737 loads from 48 states.

Delaware

Trinity Transport, Inc., Seaford, DE   P: 800-846-3400 loads 48 states.

Florida

John Green Logistics, Titusville, FL   P: 800-538-5984   F: 321-269-2340 loads out of FL to 48 states.

All-Ways Transport, Inc., Saint Petersburg, FL   P: 800-851-8801   F: 727-821-0188 loads from FL to 48 states.

Astra, Inc., Plantation, FL   P: 800-881-8123   F: 954-583-5778 LTL loads from FL to 48 states.

Intermodal Logistics, Inc., Miami, FL   P: 800-766-7778   F: 305-670-9776 loads from FL to 48 states.

Georgia

Trans Dynamics, Norcross, GA P: 800-827-7717 F: 770-921-4482 loads from GA to west coast.

Freight Shakers USA Inc., Stockbridge, GA P: 800-894-8383 F: 770-507-9713 loads from GA to mid west.

Scott Logistics Corp., Rome, GA P: 800-893-6689 F: 706-234-9141 loads from GA to MD and NJ.

DSL, Inc. Smyrna, GA , P: 1-800-267-1370 F: 770-980-9770 loads from MI to CO and west coast.

American Transp. Systems, Inc., Tucker, GA P: 800-888-2874 F: 706-561-7533 loads from GA to TX.

GTO 2000, Inc., Gainesville, GA, P: 800-966-0801 F: 770-287-7878 loads from 48 states.

Illinois

Henderson Trucking, Salem, IL P: 800-851-4943
F: 618-548-1913 loads from FL to CA.

ADM Logistics, Inc., Decatur, IL   P: 800-637-5843 F: 217-451-3278
loads from 48 states.

Sunshine Logistics Inc., Melrose Park, IL   P: 708-216-0200 F: 708-216-0206 loads from 48 states.

Freight Flow, Ltd., Bloomingdale, IL   P: 800-752-1202 F: 630-307-7400 loads from 48 states.

Seal Transportation, Inc., Hoffman Estates, IL P: 800-373-2977 F: 847-884-7300 IL to 48 states.

Indiana

USA Logistics, Inc., Chesterton, IN   P: 800-872-5999   F: 219-929-1109 load out of CO to east coast.

All Points Logistics, Inc., Indianapolis, IN   P: 317-544-1484 F: 317-544-1472 loads from 48 states.

Iowa

Ruan Transport Corp., Des Moines, IA   P: 800-493-0810 F: 515-558-3901 loads from CA and KS to west and east coast.

Norseman Transportation, Inc., Lake Mills, IA   P: 800-284-8413 F: 847-599-3070 loads from FL to mid west.

Pioneer Transfer, LLC Sioux City, IA   P: 800-325-4650 F: 712-274-2946 loads from NJ to FL.

Kansas

All Freight Brokerage, Kansas City, KS   P: 800-793-7933   F: 913-281-3338 loads from CA to mid west.

Coast to Coast Transportation Inc., Emporia, KS P: 620-342-2407 F: 620-342-3128 Loads from 48 states.

Mid-America Brokers, Kansas City, KS   P: 800-279-9142 F: 816-471-5723 loads from KS to CA.

GS Enterprises, Kansas City, KS   P: 1-877-631-1254   F: 913-543-7625 loads from CA to AZ.

Kentucky

J & J Transportation, Inc., Louisville, KY   P: 800-548-7488   F: 502-266-5176 loads from VA to west coast.

Verst Group Logistics, Walton, KY   P: 800-582-6706   F: 859-485-6285 Loads from 48 states.

Louisiana

Cargo Master Inc., Natchitoches, LA   P: 800-683-8750   F: 318-357-1732 Loads from 48 states.

Maine

ET Transportation, Palermo, ME P: 800-940-1596 F: 207-993-2839 loads from GA to ME.

North Star Transport Group Inc., Scarborough, ME   P: 800-266-9586   F: 207-885-9816 Loads from 48 states.

Maryland

Choptank Transport Inc., Preston, MD P: 800-568-2240 F: 410-673-2835 loads from NJ, PA to nationwide.

Atlantic Transportation Services, Inc., Rosedale, MD P: 800-477-8159 F: 410-406-8114 Loads from 48 states.

Massachusetts

RFX Inc., Avon, MA P: 800-342-8822 F: 508-583-3900 loads from MA and NJ to TX and west.

Allen Lund Company – Boston, MA P: 800-381-5863 F: 800-237-1622 loads from northeast to CA.

All States Transport Inc., Springfield, MA P: 800-979-9599 F: 413-739-3758 Loads from 48 states.

Michigan

VSF Transportation, Inc., Wyoming, MI P: 800-445-5623 F: 616-530-4902 loads from AZ to CA and 48 states.

RCT, Inc., Wayland, MI P: 800-677-2022 F: 616-662-2435 loads from MI to NC.

Total Logistic Control, LLC, Zeeland, MI P: 888-788-3285 F: 616-772-9903 loads from S. California to IL.

Cornerstone Systems, Grand Rapids, MI P: 800-856-7872 F: 616-791-4040 loads from CA to NH and FL.

Minnesota

Traffic Management Inc., Minneapolis, MN P: 888-726-9559 F: 763-544-3458 loads from 48 states.

Wagoneer Transportation, Inc., Eden Prairie, MN P: 800-278-0050 F: 952-833-3024 loads from OH to AZ and CA.

Online Freight Services, Inc., Mendota Heights, MN P: 800-284-2603 F: 651-468-6869 loads from FL to west coast.

Bartels Transportation Services, Inc., Winthrop, MN P: 800-422-1347 F: 612-395-9116 Loads from 48 states.

Missouri

Prime Inc, Springfield, MO P: 800-498-9268 F: 417-521-6876 loads from mid west or north east to CA.

Coastal Carriers, Inc., Troy, MO P: 877-848-8726 F: 636-528-5879 loads from CA to east coast.

UTXL, Inc., Kansas City, MO P: 800-351-2821 or 816-383-2638 loads from OH to west coast.

Nightline Express Inc., Saint Louis, MO P: 800-317-9333 F: 314-416-1660 Loads from 48 states.

Ortran, Inc., Independence, MO P: 816-373-8855 F: 816-373-8897 Loads from 48 states.

Montana

Freight Agency Inc., Billings, MT P: 800-676-6166
F: 406-245-5404 Loads from 48 states.

DTS Logistics, Billings, MT   P: 406-896-3460 F: 406-896-3490
loads from MS to west coast.

Nebraska

Grand Island Express, Grand Island, NE P: 1-800-444-9008
F: 308-384-7672 loads from IN to CO

United Dispatch Inc., Omaha, NE P: 800-228-9272
F: 402-330-5617 Loads from NE to 48 states.

New York

Trans-Pro, Champlain, NY   P: 800-463-7532   F: 866-358-9203
loads from east coast to 48 states. Also loads from CA

T.F.G. Transport, LLC, Canandaigua, NY   P: 800-396-1832 F: 585-919-0059 loads from NY to CA and to TX, LA IL.

Productive Transportation Services, Tonawanda, NY P: 800-777-5656
F: 716-877-6331 loads from NY to west coast.

Trailer Transport System, Inc., Rochester, NY   P: 585-427-2080 F: 585-427-0559 loads from NY State to West.

Logistic Dynamics, Amherst, NY   P: 800-554-3734   F: 716-250-3498 loads from MA and NH to VA.

North Carolina

Bradco Transp., Inc., Graham, NC P: 336-578-0193 F: 336-578-9026 loads from MI to GA.

Wootton Transportation, Durham, NC P: 800-222-4751 F: 919-688-2635 loads from NJ to south east.

Salem Logistics, Inc., Winston Salem, NC P: 800-326-5268 F: 336-725-5123 Loads from 48 states.

New Jersey

Genpro Transportation Services, Newark, NJ P: 1-800-243-6770 F: 973-589-1877 loads from AZ to east coast.

Paramount Freight Systems, Inc., Lodi, NJ P: 800-590-6642 F: 201-462-0507 loads from NJ to west coast.

Amodei Brokerage Co., Marlton, NJ P: 800-266-3341 F: 856-874-9240 loads from NJ to west coast.

North Dakota

Land Transportation, LLC, Fargo, ND P: 800-437-4166 F: 701-282-9760 loads from NJ, PA to west coast.

Davis Trucking Inc., Jamestown, ND P: 1-888-252-5831 F: 701-252-0282 load from PA to west coast.

Britton Transport, Inc., Grand Forks, ND P: 701-772-6681 F: 701-746-6493 loads from east coast to west.

Ohio

Total Quality Logistics, Inc., Milford, OH - P: 800-580-3101 - loads from 48 states.

BNSF Logistics, LLC, OH, P: 800-766-6870 F: 618-466-3095 loads from 48 states.

Logan Logistics LLC, Canton, OH P: 800-821-7054 F: 330-478-0557 loads from OH to CA.

Bridge Logistics, Cincinnati, OH P: 800-522-0671 F: 513-874-4161 loads from MA to west coast.

MCS – Motor Carrier Service, Northwood, Ohio - P: 800-359-9710 loads from OH to MO.

Fleet Service, Inc., Newark, OH P: 800-999-7566 loads from OH to CA.

Oklahoma

Mark Westby & Associates, Inc., Tulsa, OK P: 918-632-0010 F: 918-632-0030 loads from MI -OH -PA to southeast.

D&M Carriers, Inc., Oklahoma City, OK P: 800-645-4084 loads from CO to east coast.

Smart Lines, Oklahoma City, OK P: 866-865-4637 F: 405-848-2960 loads from OK and mid west to 48 states.

Oregon

I.C.C.I., Medford, OR   P: 800-422-8785 F: 541-734-9142
loads from CA to OR and WA

Intransit Inc., Medford, OR   P: 1-800-547-2053 F: 541-770-1399
loads from IL, MO, OR, WA to TX

K & M Distribution, Rogue River, OR P: 800-221-0182 F: 541-582-1450 loads from OR and CA to east coast.

Beaver Freight Services, LLC, Portland, OR P: 800-800-2066 F: 503-281-4773 loads from CO to east coast.

Hammell Logistics, Hermiston, OR P: 866-314-8997 F: 541-567-7607 loads from VA to west coast.

Interstate Logistics Inc., Portland, OR P: 800-860-2322 F: 503-240-6303 loads from CA to OR.

Integrity Logistics, Beaverton, OR P: 503-582-4444 F: 503-582-4445 loads from WA to CA.

Truck Transportation Services, Wilsonville, OR P: 800-632-0228 loads from OR to east coast.

Northland Express Transport, Troutdale, OR P 800-950-1010 loads from OR to East.

Hammell Logistics, Inc., Hermiston, OR P: 866-314-8997 loads from FL to CA.

Truck Transportation Services, Wilsonville, OR P: 800-632-0228 loads from OR to NC.

Pennsylvania

Mawson & Mawson Inc., Langhorne, PA P: 800-262-9766 F: 215-750-7835 loads from NJ and PA to west coast.

Trans 58, Edinboro, PA P: 800-685-7671 F: 814-734-8920 loads from PA to TX.

JR Transportation, Lancaster, PA P: 800-462-6049 F: 717-394-1600 loads from NJ to TN.

Action Cargo Freight, Hanover Township, PA P: 800-451-3158 F: 866-815-8767 loads from 48 states.

South Carolina

Gene Morris Co, Inc., Columbia, SC P: 800-232-4363 F: 803-419-5558 loads from GA to west coast and 48 states.

South Dakota

MCT Logistics LLC., Sioux Falls, SD P: 605-339-8400 F: 605-339-8449 loads from OH to TX.

Tennessee

ATS Logistics Services Inc., Brentwood, TN P: 800 338-0497 F: 615-373-5384 Loads from 48 states.

Truckload Carriers of Chattanooga, LLC, Chattanooga, TN P: 800-785-8664 F: 423-894-4550—loads from 48 states.

Cornerstone Systems, Inc., Memphis, TN P: 800-278-7677 F: 901-842-0675 Loads from 48 states.

Texas

MTS Transportation Inc., Amarillo, TX P: 806-622-8400 F: 806-622-8408 loads from Texas and Greeley CO to CA

Bertling Logistics, Inc., Houston, TX P: 800-846-8743 F: 713-490-9235 loads from TX to 48 states and inside CA.

A&A Transportation, San Antonio, TX P: 800-367-0294 F: 210-568-8907 loads from South TX to 48 states.

Bear Transportation Services, Dallas, TX P: 800-527-5380 F: 972-239-6321 loads from TX to 48.

Cargo-Master, Inc., Dallas, TX P: 800-683-8750 F: 214-428-3604 loads from TX to west coast.

Amino Transport, Inc. Hurst, TX - P: 800-842-7251 F: 817-514-3803 loads from TX to AZ.

Heyl Logistics, Edinburg, TX - P: 800-292-6778 F: 956-383-0319 loads from South Texas to CA.

Stevens Transport, Dallas, TX P: 800-347-4312 F: 502-839-8572 loads from TX to west coast.

Allen Lund, San Antonio, TX P: 800-456-5863 F: 800-477-5863 loads from TX to CO and west coast.

Swan Transportation, Tyler, TX P: 903-533-4086 F: 903-533-9742 loads from North TX, OK to east coast.

Logistic Services, Richmond, TX P: 800-214-9660 F: 832-595-8239 loads from south east to TX.

Mason Haulers, Pearland, TX   P: 866-304-3064   F: 817-545-7510   and
F: 281-992-6709
loads from AL to west coast.

Federal Transportation Systems, Inc., Houston, TX P: 800-231-0245
F: 713-464-4671 Loads from 48 states and Mexico.

Elston Nationwide Carriers, Hurst, TX P: 800-288-4314 F: 817-427-1007 loads from TX to 48 states.

JKC Enterprises, Mansfield, TX - P: 800-783-8565 F: 817-842-4210 loads from OH to TX.

Blakeman Transportation, Fort Worth, TX P: 800-375-9995 F: 817-626-0600 loads from TX to west coast.

UTAH

GTO 2000, Inc., Salt Lake City, UT   P: 866-558-3495 F: 702-564-8623 loads from CO and NV to TX and from AZ to CA. (office moved to Henderson NV)

Central Refrigerated Service, Inc., West Valley City, UT P: 800-777-9100 F: 801-924-7131 -loads from OH to CA and CO to CA.

Cargo Master Inc, Clearfield, UT P: 800-683-8750 F: 801-773-9326 Loads from 48 states.

Virginia

**Allstate Transport Services, Fredericksburg, VA P: 540-752-9698
F: 540-752-9356 Loads from 48 states.**

Washington

**Kader Co., Yakima, WA   P: 509-248-2777 F: 509-575-4942
loads from WA and OR to east coast –**

**Shippers Choice Transportation Services, Wenatchee, WA P: 800-323-8103
F: 509-663-8736 loads from 48 states.**

**Gulick Freight Services Logistics, Vancouver, WA P: 877-470-0971
F: 360-695-4787 loads from OR, WA to east coast.**

**Allen Lund, Washington State   P: 800-999-
5863   F: 360-256-4080 loads from WA and OR
to east coast.**

**Blackhorse Transportation Group, Silverdale, WA   P: 800-800-
7136 F: 360-638-0874 loads from WA , OR to east coast.**

**Associated Freight Brokers, Yakima, WA   P: 800-548-
0669 F: 509-575-6555 loads from TX to west coast.**

Wisconsin

**Elite Freight Solutions LLC, Manitowoc, WI   P: 920-686-8200
F: 920-682-3097 loads from OR and CA to east coast.**

**M2 Logistics Inc., Green Bay, WI P: 920-569-8801 F: 920-569-8843
Loads from 48 states.**

**Northern Freight Service, Inc., Middleton, WI P: 800-383-8688
F: 608-836-4070 Loads from 48 states.**

TruckingSuccess.com

7054 North 28th Drive
Phoenix, AZ 85051
Tel. (602) 864-8056
support@truckingsuccess.com

*Information presented in this brochure is current at the time of printing.
Specifications subject to change.*
TXu1-335-556
Copyright 2020 TruckingSuccess.com All Rights Reserved.

www.ingramcontent.com/pod-product-compliance
Lightning Source LLC
Chambersburg PA
CBHW081659220526
45466CB00009B/2822